AYRSHIRE RECESSIONAL

GORDON JARVIE

AYRSHIRE RECESSIONAL

AND OTHER POETRY

HARPER*croft*

EDINBURGH 1998

IN MEMORIAM
Daisy Beattie Jarvie
1909-1996

First published 1998

Harpercroft Books

81 Comiston Drive

Edinburgh EH10 5QT

Scotland

ISBN 0 9533530 0 1

Book designed by Mark Blackadder

Printed by Bookcraft (Bath) Ltd

Cover illustration: 'Catterline in winter', Joan Eardley
(reproduced by kind permission of the Scottish National Gallery of Modern Art)

CONTENTS

Compass bearings: Troon

I watch the red disk of a languorous
sun's slow lapse below a western sea
off the far end of Academy Street.
Rightward the sleeping bulk of Arran.

Stars dot a darkening sky to south
above the slighter mass of Merrick,
a toenail moon etching itself from nowhere.
Orion the hunter strides out, sharp and clear.

East by Dundonald Hill a fuzzier view,
the blinds of dusk already well drawn down.
But my mind's eye picks out a court's musicians
rehearse their notes and play at Harpercroft.

North is the shortest view from where I stand,
but once again the mind's eye pictures it –
ducks flying firthward over a silent strand
and a white dune fade-out into a sloe-black night.

How many ocean tides have lapped and ebbed,
how many far-off flaming suns have set
upon this scene?

The mighty fallen

                    Once,
she took us with her
everywhere. Now
it takes two of us
to take her anywhere.

                    Then,
everything achieved at speed,
as if dear life depended on it.
Half-dragging our wee arms
from their poor sockets,
fleeing with us up the station brae
through slanting stinging rain,
shackled to her wake –
the only way for her to catch a train
was by the skin of her teeth,
shouting at startled railwaymen
to 'Hold that train!'

We inch along so slowly now,
one dragging foot at a time,
getting there, more or less,
pulling along with stick or zimmer frame.
But it is wonderful to see her smile
and watch her travel hopefully
in her inimitable and indomitable style,
even if subsided in that chair,
that nest of rugs and cushions.

She used to be so strict with us,
applying well aimed slap or noisy scold.
Now in turn we have to be so firm with her,
and wrap her up against encircling cold
if we are going to take her anywhere.

Larger than life

The hard bit
is watching loved ones
diminished
who were once
so much larger than life;

whose lives once shone
(we like to think)
to enlighten our darkness
themselves flickering
and dimming towards their dusk.

For then we know
it's our turn
to raise our game
and throw our afternoon light
into their shadows –

trying to bring them
out of their soul's dark night.
The big fear then is this: Will
our batteries be strong enough
to see them through?

Barnweil Hill, by Craigie

Then : 1296

Distant defiance of blue Arran hill,
white mirror slash of water in the sun,
an airy sky goes whistling by,
the Barns o Ayr burn weel, quo I,
where Braveheart went in for the kill.

There fell the English governor of Ayr
with his lippy bumptious myrmidons.
The patriot Wallace dished out justice there
and even the town's friar deaf to their orisons –
for hadn't they just tricked and slaughtered Scotia's sons?

Now : 1996

Today four of us sit in the car
by a whitewashed hilltop farm
and a tree-girt sandstone monument:
two old ladies enjoy the summer view,
a boy itches to explore it all, and I.
A lazy dog in the farmyard barks,
the blue sky fills with the singing of larks,
life tiptoes by.

A notice regrets the Wallace Tower is shut,
but the farmer has slung a long rope swing
from a high-branched elm nearby. So,
good as it might have been to climb that stair,
the boy from the car wastes little time to show
a better way up through the lark-filled air
to celebrate the deeds of Braveheart, the hero.

Swan Lake, by Culzean

For some reason, my walks here seem
uncannily remembered, clear as last night's dream.

So much else forgotten, somehow they
get kept and kept, and are not thrown away.

The last time: an early summer afternoon,
sunny and warm, a-buzz with bees in June.

In a distant field a flock of – surely not? – ostriches;
big and black and white, ridiculous as witches.

You in the wheelchair urged me along,
unperturbed by muddy paths or approaching swan.

The time before, we walked. You took frequent seats and an arm
apiece from Andrew and me. It was thundery and warm.

Longer ago, we tried out binoculars and a red pushchair
here. That day, his big sister was the passenger.

Once with Dad here, I had a brisk and serious talk
about What I Would Do With My Life. That was a winter walk.

One teenage springtime I sat here under birch trees
with my valentine. We heard heartbeats in the breeze.

Far-away childhood picnics I can just about recall
playing the livelong day here, earliest memories of all.

Will there be further visits here, alone or with folk I cherish?
I don't know. But these snapshots neither dull nor perish.

Home

Going there to visit her on Sundays,
giving the week's account of myself
and hearing bits of hers: for years it was
our regular parent–child exchange.

Thus even yesterday
thirty-odd winters after quitting the parental nest
it was still a place
I sometimes called home.

Today it's just a little Ayrshire town
because she who I'd foolishly begun
to believe to be immortal
left us last night.

Dundonald Hill

In November we sat here
watching a wintry sunset –
blues, yellows, eerie pinks
stretching far beyond Kintyre
away and away and away.

I took some photos for you that day,
no one in them, just the view
from this, your favourite vantage point
of many a year. After your weekly shop,
you used to like to sit with Dad here
and drink in that scene, light playing
across the surface of the varying firth –
sometimes seething in a westerly gale,
sometimes becalmed . . .

It's nearly Christmas now.
This morning I sit here alone
and at my back a winter sun creeps up.
Rays feel their speculative ways
through blue-grey haze
and probe towards the sea.

Right now they are invisible but I know
that Arran's peaks are over there;
leftward is Ailsa Craig, and then
the tapering Carrick Hills
and Heads of Ayr.

And if I shut my eyes a moment
hard against the misty glare
and steady myself, I know
you too are here again,
just as we were.

Arran, from Troon

OZYMANDIAS IN AIRDRIE

Once long ago my Grandpa Beattie
took me by tram out to the country
past Airdrie, I think. We took a walk there
past a colossal building, boarded up.

Aged about eight, I asked what it was. He said
it had been the biggest blotting-paper factory
in the whole world, but closed since folk had recently
gone from using ink pens to biros overnight.

I know from the rhyme that an ink-dipped pen
was a boon and a serious blessing to men
and to blotting-paper factories, but why oh why
didn't these folk anticipate trends and diversify?

Did they watch a moving finger write
and having writ move on? Did they lack wit to see
that factories are valued not for what they make
but what they sell? Or did they see, and their hands shake?

Who knows – poor sad turkeys failing to escape
Christmas, harbingers of a post-industrial landscape.
Why did my grandpa take me for that walk?
Too late now to ask, too late for talk. This I recall:

Our horror at lost jobs was palpable, at a village's despair
at nothing left to do. I picture still sclerosis and decay
creep over that redundant workshop, silent and bare,
where a lone and windswept hillside drops away.

GRANDMA

Veteran player of an endless street,
she seems to own the thronging crowd
we pass among and through.

Clasping some stranger's hand
she often comes away
with awesome civilities
which I can only whisper half-aloud:
'Sure, but you're looking great.
Can it be twenty years since last I saw ye?'

Aged half of that, I wholly fail
to grasp how she can possibly recall
so long the look of someone's face.
Do time or memory not alter them?
Are they indelible?

Yesterday I lunched with a man
I hadn't seen for twentysomething years,
and suddenly I was thinking again
about the magisterial assurance
of those greetings and perambulations,
those throwaway lines of repartee.
Grandma, would you not be proud of me
now that I too have survived this long?

Twenty years? Twenty quid?
A child and a fool imagine
they'll never be spent. Truly,
of all the things that happen to a person,
old age is the most unexpected.

AT FIRST SIGHT

A plain wooden bench up on a clifftop walk,
alone you sit there, gazing away and away
over and beyond a distant sea.

I come alongside
and you smile at me.
Nothing is said, or needs to be.

Walking that way another time I find
I'm detouring around by that windy parade
in the hope of a second sighting.

And when against the gale you do stroll into view,
I so mistrust my own two eyes that I
must pinch myself and sit down on the grass,
because my heart is seething like the elements.

This time you saunter up and sit with me.
Alone we sit and look upon a boiling sea.

THE FAIRY THORN TREE

In those more innocent times
before the latest Troubles
I hitched to country places
like Dungiven.

On arrival, driven
to the very door – 'No trouble, son' –
you are quizzed at length
about your driver. Would that
be Maguire the vet
or his brother Joe from up the Feeny road
by Knockan Bridge?
It isn't nosiness so much
as plain proof of country living
where everybody knows everybody
whatever their 'persuasion'.

On the Saturday afternoon,
a sunny windy day,
the rector takes us shooting, his son and I.
To my surprise, the man turns out
a dead-eye shot, and him a clergyman.
He bags as many snipe in half an hour
as I'd caught mackerel a month before
a mile out of Troon harbour with my dad.

Afterwards, striding across a blustery moor
behind a house called Pellipar he takes great pride
in showing me an ancient skeagh-bush –
a squat and stunted little blackthorn tree
stuck in a shallow hollow

at the dead centre of nowhere,
but so decked out with bits of rag and cloth
that it appears a strange lost Christmas thing
beached on a summer strand.

Some of its rags are leprous and snot-green,
so it is not a thing of mystery
or beauty – rather just a scabby emblem
to a folk superstition
that still flourishes hereabouts
when nobody is looking.

Sunday turns out a busy day
for a country rector, even one
semi-retired 'from active combat'.
My host – surely in great demand? –
appears to spend his day driving about
to this or that outpost of his faith
for communion or evensong
or some other celebration.
I wonder idly if any of the churches
where he performs
might have decked themselves out
as fervently and tastelessly
as that little fairy thorn tree.

Coda

Twentysomething years on
from that weekend in another country –
or was it in another world? –
I sit in the morning bustle of a street cafe

somewhere off London's Piccadilly
sipping cappuccino while I make
urgent, last-minute preparations
for a strategic business meeting
of such paramount importance
that I've long forgotten what it was about.

Then across that cafe's hum and two decades
I hear a voice I know – English vowels
in a swirl of Irish mist, and I recognise
the speech of my one-time school friend,
the Ulster rector's son. Hailing him, I say,
'You're a long way from the fairy thorn tree.'

The startled head swings round to face me
with quickly dawning grin. 'Och aye,'
he mimicks in his best stage Scots,
'It has to be, it cannae be ither
than my auld freend Rabbie Burns,
the Ayrshire plooman.' We shake hands . . .

ONE NIGHT IN DUBLIN

A cold and wintry snap,
a light frosting of snow
dusts the dozing town
under a prescient yellow moon.

On such evenings –
even on Fridays –
the warmth of the Reading Room
is almost an attraction
and I get stuck in
to my 'Pilgrim's Progress'.

Tonight a muffled restlessness
disturbs the studious calm.
Is it me, hankering for a wild weekend,
or is there something else?

Ten o'clock. A bell rings, so soon.
A tide of students
ebbs from a round room,
returns borrowed books
and seeps out into the white crispness
of Front Square.

I pause and light a cigarette.
A friend asks, through the gloom,
Did you hear? Hear what? I ask,
recalling the uneasy ripples
across the Reading Room
and the knelling bell. A doom?

We talk, and then go separate ways.
I, in a blank daze
enter a pub to watch it all
on a merciless blue screen
high on a bar-room wall.

Old Bartkus buys me a beer.
I sip at it, trying to take this story in.

From Vanity Fair,
beyond Doubting Castle
and across the River of Death,
with all his marks and scars
Mr President has today passed over.
Today the trumpets sounded for him
upon the other side.

Looking around this room
I read one thought
on every silent face and taut
now he is gone from Camelot:
Who will fight Giant Despair for us now
and help us through this dark shadow?

Postscript, 1997

This poem happened many years ago
as I began to weigh the passing years.
It describes a spasm of my world's soul
even farther back in time. It is
a yellowing snapshot of a young man's tears.

A life's defining moments don't recede. Today
is a sunny summer morning thirty-four years on
from that far-off distress. An older man
and world wake up to learn
of another violent death.

This death of a princess is a strange demise.
A chauffeur-driven butterfly caught in a gyre
has flown inexorably at a funeral pyre
of her own creation, intoxicated
on the oxygen of her own publicity,
an accident dying to happen,
hoist on her own petard.

Another of their mother's photo opportunities,
I pity her poor children now bereft. I pity too
an older generation impelled to remember
a wintry night in November
so very long ago.

TWO SIDES OF A COIN

I remember the smiling centenarian,
rather doddery getting into his church pew,
the crumpled dark suit, the whiff of nicotine
and stale urine, the fondness for children,
the fitful flickers of an old-time disciplinarian.

She remembers a big black cloud of a dominie
who seventy years before, and more,
had personally intervened to ensure
she got six of the best for a careless slip-up
in her Gaelic-to-English translation . . .

Hearing of his death I mutter
something inane and condoleatory.
But a dark shadow passes across her gaze
before she takes a deep breath, and zestfully
pronounces the world a better place without him.

REDCURRANTS

Was it the redcurrants and perhaps
the time of year: a September day,
fine, sunny, clear, but with a tang
of winter sharpnesses to come?

Such days are bright jewels in our archives,
whatever else they are.

I recall the clean taste of the fruit
and their crimson perfection under nets
as we walked round a walled garden
on a hillside behind Innerleithen.

But like a small black cloud
across the Tweed over by Traquair
I recall too some background shadow
from which we were emerging,
and which seemed to make
a bright day even brighter,
leaving us free to focus once more
on the next steps of our journey –
at last no weight on our minds,
and once again, thank God,
no sleepless nights.

Redcurrants
remind me how good life can be.

BONFIRE

What is it that's so right about a bonfire,
drawing us moth-like to its naked flame?
Is it the standing and gazing at it,
blank, pensive, dizzy, empty –
so purposefully idle that you spin before it,
one with the spinning world?
Its sparking ember rockets bring you to.

Is it the burning up a summer's garden rubbish,
making waste places straight?
Is it that special smell
of leaf and woodsmoke
carried on clothes and hair?

An autumn nip is on the air,
thin sun hazy on turning leaves –
less yellow fruitiness
than wan reminder of summers
going their sundry ways.

Wan? Not really so.
A little blue perhaps the smoke,
but my small helpers zing with energy,
darting about with red and glowing twigs.
Their growing shadows dance around the fire.

The clocks go back tonight.
We win an hour from Father Time
as winter is declared – official.
Here is an hour in hand, and
Halloween is just a week away.
Mist, witches, broomsticks, turnip lanterns –
a special time of year.

An hour, a week, a year?
Well, Old Man Time, I watch my childish helpers,
and it's as if you give me back a lifetime
in the flash and crack of a sparking branch,
in a zonked-out smoky stare
at the fixed point
in the red heart of a fire
about thirty years ago.

FLORA

All day I sit in the meeting
and they talk and talk.
The hee-haw Oxbridge voices rise and fall.
I watch the lips move but their words fail me.
My thoughts are many miles away
where you prepare to make your lifetime's trip.

Please take things gently, please take care.
Will you be gone, will you be there
when I get home?

You played so many parts in all our lives –
friend, neighbour, parent, granny, seasoned guide.
Flora, I have so much to thank you for,
and there is nothing now that I can do
to spare you what I know
you're going through.

'I need to pack it in,' you said,
'I'm weary now. It won't go on much more.'
My heart fell to the floor to hear those words,
although I knew how very right you were.

We sat and listened to the clock awhile.
Nothing was said, and everything.
I held your hand, and thought of all those tins
of baby food downstairs that morning,
wondering would you even manage to eat that.

'Stay with us as long as you can,' I brought
myself to say in feeblest way.
'Now who will eat the baby food?' I thought.

REFLECTION

I like to look in shop windows
sometimes. It costs nothing.
Nobody tries
to sell you stuff or hassle you
with 'How may I help you?'
or 'Something you require?'

Stroll up the street,
stop where you desire,
stand and stare – wineshops
are good sometimes,
and it can take me half an hour
to navigate a bookshop window.

You sometimes get surprises
even in shop windows: yesterday I did.
Coat collar upturned,
who was that wispy old scruff
loitering in the street behind me,
reflected in the window pane?

Turning around to see who's there,
I laugh a hollow laugh
as bitter-sweet I hear the penny drop.
Aweel, I sigh, that really is no gift
to see myself as others do,
reflected in the window of this shop.

Is that faceless old scarecrow really me?
No, it is not in me but vainly
in my children that I like to see
myself. They are still young
and beautiful.

BORN LOSER

Five words are the querulous refrain
of such a hopeless person:
'Has *any*body seen my specs?'

He leaves his gloves or hat upon the train,
'mislays' his file of research at the library,
once – most grievously – lost his wedding ring,

is known not seldom to become
strangely detached from scarf and other things;
only last week contrived to lose a wallet

and all the personal stuff therein: the plastic
cheque cards, membership IDs
and various open sesames –

the vital formal detritus
of an ongoing existence, besides an oh–
so-precious photo of his daughter as a child.

Long ago, maybe worst of all, within five minutes
of first setting foot in New York, he was 'relieved'
of a suitcase containing his very core –

a file stuffed with a decade's poems,
his twenties wiped out in the time it took
to ask directions for Stony Brook,

Long Island. Later, he was to reach his destination
still shaking. Even today I shake
at the memory of it.

BEFORE IT ALL BEGINS AGAIN

Some mornings, lying awake
and listening to the intensity
of silences before the clocks go off
and everything begins again,
it's as if I hear a taxi
waiting at the front door,
its engine running quietly.

And I lie there
thinking, 'Can it be
time's wingèd chariot?

Again? Already?'

TADPOLES

More than
a nine days' wonder,
they are a yearly miracle.

The spawn a sign
of frogs' benison,
an annual visitation.

The jerking, wriggling
black question marks
pose their eternal why.

We witness their cycle
through a hindsight of years,
a shrug of tears.

Their formlessness assumes
such precise shape, follows
such predestined sequence.

The back legs minuscule,
the disappearing tail,
the swelling 'head' –

then suddenly front legs
and – presto! – wee frogs,
entirely perfect of form.

We encourage them, of course,
if only in the pious hope
of seeing quivering blobs of spawn

again, another year; and for the joy
of saying another time,
'Guess what's appeared in the pond!'

Winter day, Indiana

Through these ice-patterned window-panes I stare.
We meet, the world and I, on this cold sill.
Across my breath, out of this whitened air
I first smell blood run chill.

Winters here are grey. Even grass
when it appears is grey after the snows.
Streets, faces, sidewalks, feelings – all are grey,
and skies are heavy, leaden, and foreclosed.

Spring, in an Edinburgh park

Livid dappled greenwood scene,
buds of May bursting with urgency,
sharp, foliage fresh, and squeaky clean –
in beryl, emerald, lime, aquamarine,
a dozen verdant shades of tingling green.

Then after rain, the pungent, rutty smells,
the hint of sap and undergrowth –
of garlic crushed and spunky hint
of hawthorn, tang of campion and sloe,
the unfurling evolution of the ferns.

Here now is fullness, an effulgent whiff
to keep a 'grand parfumier' sharp of nose.
Here is a riotous rapture to sustain
Van Gogh, Cézanne, or Matisse on tiptoes
straining to make art approach this artless scene,
this greenwood's fragrant flaunting of the green.

LOSS

Emerging from the kirk
with my family
into a howling wind,
someone observed
my tear-stained cheek
and asked me
what was on my mind.

Nothing much, I replied.
I am merely lamenting
the long-lost certainties
of my childhood.

BUT WHAT'S IT *for*?

For some considerable time
she stands and looks at it.
Next she runs off a little way
and then comes back,
pursing her lips,
giving the thing
her quantity surveyor look
and frowning her quizzical appraisal,
hanging her head to one side,
then shaking it hard –
maybe in disbelief?

Next comes the tactile approach
as she rubs her hands
across the shiny silver
of its flat rippling surfaces,
then taps it,
listens awhile,
and smacks it hard.

Is that a satisfying noise
which appeals to her? Maybe.
Inspecting for some time contentedly,
she smacks it here and there.

Finally she looks at me and asks,
'What is it?' And I say,
'A sculpture.' Then the harder question,
'But what's it *for*?' (her emphasis).
And I reply, 'For looking at.'

Unsatisfied with my answer perhaps
as only a three-year-old can be,
she thumps it again, hard as she can.

THE STAYING POWER OF PLANTS

Aged about two,
with muddy but triumphant gardener's face,
I remember the day
you didn't so much plant it
as shove it in its tiny flowerpot,
not into a prepared soil but
into your gooey mud-pie mix.

Like you it throve.
It several times outgrew its little pot,
but I could never bring myself
to throw out 'Sally's plant'. It has
no other name for me. I only know
I have repotted it four or five times
just as I did today into
more spacious quarters,
more room to grow.

Like you its roots have always
nicely filled the space provided.
Like you it now stands tall.
But though it does not flower –
does not do *any*thing but grow –
I have to grant it is
my favourite household plant.
That is because it is for me
a little evergreen offshoot
of your innocence.

Also I begin to see
that it will be here still,
long after you
have spread your wings.

Thus do I realise it's wrong of me
to underestimate the sheer longevity,
the earthbound staying power
of plants.

PTERODACTYL

For Wilma Horsbrugh

This is the tale of a pterodactyl
extinct for quadrillions of years.
 It slept frozen stiff
 at the foot of a cliff
un-noticed, or so it appears.

And then the climate got warmer,
causing the icecap to thaw,
 till the ice round it broke
 and the creature awoke,
astonished by all that it saw.

At first it remained quite immobile.
Then suddenly, after a week,
 'I'd better get moving,'
 it muttered – thus proving
pterodactyls are able to speak.

The folk of St Leonards that morning,
got a horrible frightening surprise,
 when something enormous came stumbling
 down the cragside quite audibly mumbling –
a *thing* of incredible size!

The creature tried to be friendly
so its feelings were dreadfully hurt
 when the folk ran away.
 Then they all heard it say,
'Humans treat pterodactyls like dirt.'

The poor thing, although it took umbrage,
persevered in its efforts to charm them.
    But by wagging its tail
    it created a gale –
most dramatic, and bound to alarm them.

'St Leonards folk,' mused the creature,
'Were hostile to me from the start.
    And it's only too clear
    that I'm not wanted here.
I'd be wiser, I'm sure, to depart.

'This earth I'm obliged to abandon.
To Mars I shall fly, and quite soon.
    On second thoughts not,
    for Mars is too hot.'
So it set off that night for the moon.

And space travellers now in the Nineties
on the moon have observed a new feature.
    For there frozen stiff
    in a vast lunar cliff
they've discovered a curious creature –

                a pterodactyl!

EGYPT

Everyone asked
what I thought of the pyramids.

I said,
I saw schools and classrooms,
teachers giving English from textbooks
to classfuls of eager children
slightly unsure of our presence,
too polite to come right out
and ask what we were doing there.
But they plainly wondered
had we come to inspect them?

Much welcoming: bowing and smiling,
shaking of hands, quite formal.
That is the end of the lesson,
most of the teachers say, as if
to suggest we can go now.
What happens then, I wonder –
not that I'm much good at being
a fly on the wall of another culture.
Spectator sports
were never my strongest card.

Traffic-clogged streets
and trips to the ministry. Armed outriders
and wailing escorts and then
the official car. That was
the minister, someone whispers.
Such style. But that is it –
that's as near as we get. Ministers are

too high-powered and armour-plated
for the likes of us. So we sit
with the English Counsellor
for more smiles and words of welcome;
and little cups of karkaday to sip –
a red drink, sweet and refreshing,
made from dried flowers of hibiscus.

The draft proposal is sketched
for the Counsellor's approval. We wait to see;
and then the nod, the smile, the invitation
to come back tomorrow, and discuss
matters in more depth. Good – this is success,
this is what we came for.

                    Outside the town,
the sphinx smiles on into another sunset,
the wonders of an ancient world unvisited yet.

And the pyramids? I don't know,
I said. I haven't seen them yet.

ON FIRST LOOKING INTO
THE PACIFIC OCEAN

That day I stared at Pacific's wide expanse,
silent, from a wee hill in Valparaiso
scanning the horizon of the Spanish Main
for realms of gold, for goodly states and kingdoms.
It looked to me like any other hazy glimpse of sea
viewed from a certain distance: the English Channel, say,
seen from the Kemptown racecourse, or maybe
the Firth of Forth from somewhere up behind Dunbar
where Cromwell wrought his havoc once.

Later, leaving Chile on an eighteen-hour flight
from Santiago, is ample time to tell myself
that official British export missions, replete
with formal receptions at the embassy –
First Commercial Attaché holding court here
(posing under shimmering cut-glass chandelier),
Under-Secretary of something-or-other glittering there
(polished foot resting on gilt-paint Empire chair) –
are perhaps not the ideal location in which
to be caught nodding over Chapman's Homer.

THE BEACH AT ACCRA

Blaze of steel-grey sea, shimmering splash of sand,
warm breeze blowing from sea to land.
A bunch of holy rollers, drenched in pious ecstasy,
throw themselves about the blistering strand,
moaning, lowing, bellowing deliriously,
looking as if they might do themselves
some less-than-godly injury.

Slow fisherfolk sort massive nets, and go about
livelihoods with careful, biblical consideration.
Visiting folk, from hotels or airlines, sit in shade
sipping atmosphere, club cocktails, lazy syncopation
to strains of Ebenezer Obay and his Dark City Sisters.
Myself, and a scatter of intrepid souls, heave out
in a massive surf, shrieking
at the white noonday enormity of it all.

Moored offshore two bluish outlines, cargo boats,
brought out the early morning crowds
and queues of ever-hopeful shoppers.
The shops are out of oil and soap
and I don't know what. What's the hope
for a place where oil-palm grows wild, and they can't
supply their own market needs?

That evening at the hotel, declining wine I spread
imported Dutch butter on my bread, and learn
it's all a false alarm. The boats are empty –
a mirage. No stocking up in town today.

THE EDITOR SALUTES JANET OGBO

For Ron Heapy

I
Bright as a button, big-eyed,
keen as mustard, slate in hand,
you walk three miles in the cool
of the morning to your bush school.
Pondering to ingest a day's wisdom,
you then walk back the same three miles
in the torpor of a Takoradi afternoon in Ghana.

Braided hair teased out by loving hands,
neat in blue cotton dress and sandals,
you carry on your head your case of books
as if it were the crown jewels of Asante
or an unexploded bomb-cluster of western learning.

II
For nigh on thirty years, hacking a way
through the jungle of a thousand texts
and endless books, I picture you
in a clear mind's eye. Always the question is
the same: 'What would Janet Ogbo make of this?'

The usual answer – 'Not a lot!' – means stripping
the text back to basics, simplifying it perhaps,
clarifying messages, cutting out fancy bits,
pruning digressions within digressions,
paring away tricks, amplifying the drift
where brambling verbiage hides the textual path –
until such time as one and all can say,
'*Now* is the meaning plain!'

III
Dear Janet, would you be amused to know
that you are still – for me – as you first started out,
a bonny twelve-year-old schoolgirl? My mind
rejects the notion that your own children
have been through school, and now are busy
raising babies of *their* own. Like an old photo,
my memory keeps you as you always were for me.

How are you coping, Janet Ogbo, after all these years?
Across two continents and three decades I salute you.

NIGERIAN FLASHBACK

We cross the bridge into Onitsha,
my Yoruba friend and I.
He fearful of his reception,
a war only just resolved;
I – his cover – also watchful,
my first trip to former Biafra.
Will anyone want to see us?
Will they be hostile or friendly?
Are we too soon to do business?

One end of the bridge still down,
a pontoon contraption there. The road
from the Niger up the long hill to town
showing plenty of signs of action –
craters, buildings pocked with gunshot,
some baldy looking palm trees
lying at palm-wine drunken angles . . .
We wonder how it has been,
and who has survived.

First port of call the old CMS bookshop
to seek out Mr Nwankwo.
It's just as it was, says my Yoruba friend.
Look at their wonderful textbooks.
Where did all this come from?
Who paid for all this, he wonders
aloud, as I follow him through
the darkened cool of the warehouse.

Oh greetings Olaiya, comes the call
from the green depths of the building.
Then they seem to fall on each other:
much hugging and patting of backs,
loud rolls of deep laughter, they
walk about holding hands,
perhaps afraid to lose touch again
with each other.

Congratulations, man, you survived,
is the gist of the conversation.

Coda

Later, I learned what had happened,
after the death of my Yoruba friend,
he and I that had travelled in Igboland
and been made welcome and feted
in erstwhile enemy territory.

One day, among his own people,
for so-called political reasons,
he was doused in petrol and set alight
in front of his wife and children.
Pray for his outraged soul's repose.

He had backed the losing side
in an irascible election campaign,
forgetting man's fathomless savagery.
So a volatile mob of his townsmen
went to his house and did that to him.

ROGER

Today I saw Roger,
but not my Roger. It shook me
to see that look on him, not his.
I knew he'd been unwell, but not
until I saw him did I realise
how many rounds he'd gone
with the grim reaper,
and that he wasn't
looking forward to another bout.

A day at a time, he said,
which is fair comment.
I nodded. We shook hands
with some emotion, and I knew
that he was holding on.

Then we helped him into his taxi
and my old friend was gone.

KISS

From that white sepulchre his bed
he held a gaunt cheek up,
but it was twenty years
since I had kissed him last.
Thus – when it mattered much – I failed
to pick his plaintive signal up.

With gestured smile, handclasp, and wave,
I left the bed numb and unthinking. But
driving home I understood, heart sinking,
the meaning of that grave gesture,
and realised how ultimately
I had betrayed him.

These moments cannot be rehearsed,
they are disastrous and unbearable.
There is no second shot at them.

SCOTS ACCENT

After the talk, in some
unlikely place like Wimbledon,
a lady from the audience came to bray:
'I lurved your accent. I could've
listened to it all day.'

My response was less impertinent
than quizzically meant. I said:
'Never mind how I speak, my deah.
Did you by any chance get to heah
what I was trying to say?'

NATIONALITY

'Nationality?' asks
the uniformed customs man
from behind
his glass screen.

'British,' I mouth
into the bullet-proof fishtank.

Fingering my passport as if
it is a thing distasteful,
unclean, even infectious,
he turns to a uniformed
colleague and hisses at him,
'Engleesh.'

                'No, no,' I enunciate
back at him. 'Scottish.'

'Oh, move along,' he growls
with dark Levantine frown,
drawing from some deep well
of despotic irritation.
'Can't you see
that we're busy?'

COLLEAGUE: A SKETCH

Warrior matriarch, something between
Ma Slessor and old Boudicca the queen,
she revels in her woman's burdens
and attends her flagging myrmidons.

Are they still wet behind the ears,
this brood of hers? She steers
them cheeping through the undergrowth,
away from ambush
by some lurking quango
fearful for its poxy territory.

In the background –
strictly off the record, of course,
gnats, gadflies, sniping mandarins
and clouds of civil servants buzz about
with gaping unconvincing grins,
covering their flanks,
disclaiming responsibility
if anything goes wrong,
shuffling their papers.
Lethally inscrutable.

Through it all
she exhorts with winning smile
from faltering foot soldiers
one extra mile.

Face soft with the afterglow
of Christmas, she informed
me how she'd become a grandmother
again. I saw the warrior transformed,

domestic matriarch to a younger brood,
offering piggy-backs under a tinsel tree,
hunkered down behind a sofa
for hide-and-seek.

Will her babies recall these festal scenes
when they are gangling
through their gawky teens?
They may remember the enthusiast
who shared high days and holidays with them,
the hundred percenter, the person
who was not mealy-mouthed,
was not a half-measures person,
someone who filled a room.

But will they ever know
hers was the face
that ran a Scottish Office roadshow
and launched a thousand project writers?

And I? Pianissimo, I
am a sort of second clarinet
seconded to the vast symphony orchestra
where she is resident conductor. I
go to her for help with my score,
which mercifully she knows,
and gives.

10 July

Today we lie abed listening to country noises.
A rooster crows, quite loud, on nearby hill.
Another answers further off –
and then another one, just audible.
A distant dog barks. Someone is sawing wood
a mile or so away.
Rising at noon, I plant my mimosa tree,
all three trembling feet of her,
in the shade of our hazel clump and of the little oak.
At lunch we open a bottle of Cramoisay
to handsel this addition to our landscape.

Today is the first day of our holiday,
and it is hot.

13 July

Where to go?
In all the villages
a late-night *bal musette* and firework show.
slow, slow, quick-quick slow.

By Langon church a wired-up, microphoned chanteuse
is belting out the numbers while the booze
flows freely from a huckster's makeshift stall
under a warm and inky sky – *la belle étoile.*
Today – *la veille du quatorze juillet.*

We drive on through the sticky, moth-live dark
to Beslé by the river and the park.
Here too the kids are all up late to see
the fireworks and festivity.

At midnight to loud gasps along the quay
we get what we have all stayed up to see –
the flares, the flashes and the shooting stars,
the noisy firecracks and the jollity.

A smoky, sulphurous, enchanting whiff
pervades the winking fairylights.

19 July

In shimmering heat
today they cut the yellow wheat.
The shards of dusty chaff and gritty stoor
fly through the open windows and the door
and now lie thick and deep
upon our unswept kitchen floor.

25 July

Last night we watched a lightning storm
dance over and light up our flashing skies.
For half an hour we stood and gawped
at entertainment not available on Sky TV
and were reminded of our littleness.

In a strange half-dark it started
away to the south, like heavy breathing
far off in front of the house
and over the maize fields. A sudden coolness,
distant drums of thunder, searing flashes
and zigzag lights – pinks, yellows, greens,
quiet at first, then louder, closer, *here*,
as gusts of rain began to shake the trees
with plopping spots of wet. And then,
better than Beethoven,
the blatter and crashing overhead.

We watched, then hugged each other for a while,
as our ancestors would have done
at such a scary thing. Then a farewell sigh,
and just as suddenly as it came, it passed
away to the north behind the house,
and we ran through to watch it disappear
rumbling over the valley ridge of our world.

Andrew did a raindance then, for relief,
on the dark road. We heard only
the downpipes from our roof gargoyling water.
Our waterbarrels, empty, dry, hot this afternoon,
now overflowing. And overhead –
bats in a cooler, moonlit sky. And everywhere
the sweet, slaked smell of quenching earth
and of deep-drinking hazel trees.

28 July

Aren't the acorns here voluptuous,
round and full and green –
and in July too.
Not the scrunty wee things
that pass for acorns in Scotland
in late September.

29 July

Slowly, I'm digging a ditch in front of the house,
a run-off channel for those fierce flash-floods
you get here after thunder and lightning.
Maybe it'll make some sort of patio
one day. Who knows?

The postman thinks I'm mad
to work in such a heat. *Un mercénaire,*
he calls me with a shake of the head.
Urging caution, he leaves a letter
and drives off in his yellow car.
Sweating copiously, I dig another metre
then pause for breath and beer.

30 July

We know that Paris is on holiday now.
There are hairdos in the village, and gold sandals,
and men with handbags. There were two
of them at the baker's this morning.

I caught the heavenward-glancing shrugs,
the slightest Gallic upping of an eyebrow
between two elderly locals,
which said it all.

4 August

Summer wholeness,
our valley world
now ripe to its core,
trees full and green and fruiting,
yellow fields sighing with corn,
maize stems well formed.

The world fixed and still,
the house snoozing,
I step outside to watch dusk's onset
as long blue shadows slide
into the dim husk of night
beneath a ghosting moon.

I jump. A phantom grey moth
careers with sudden bump
against my forehead,
veering into a velvet sky
and the soft silent jaw
of an approaching bat.

12 August

The megaliths scattered over the heath at Saint-Just
are white teeth in a shimmering heat.
Never exactly busy this last three thousand years,
we have them to ourselves this morning.

Today we show them to the cousins
who climb on them. They enjoy
the shaded rockface at Le Val,
conveniently replete
with piton-ringed metal spikes
to take their ropes.

Below, across the gleaming water of the lake
the streaking blue of kingfishers.

THE DAY WE SAW THE CONGER

For Jamie, who saw it first, but not that day

Sometimes a conger eel
is longer than a man
and thicker than his upper arm.
With bulldog gargoyle head
it is a deep-sea creature
ugly and black as sin,
shiny and alligator strong,
something to haunt a child's dreams
for a year or two.

This one was all of the above and more,
and it presumed to stray
too close inshore that summer day,
lurking on a tide-wracked channel's floor
among dark jagged rocks
and swaying fronds of weed.

Moving against the ocean's flow
just once too often,
it drew attention to itself
and frantic met its fate:
a weekend snorkel fisherman's harpoon
between the staring eyes.

The seething struggle which ensued
matched two noble antagonists.
The wounded eel thrashed furiously,
trying to unskewer itself
and turn on its attacker.

Keeping the harpoon arrow
at careful arm's length,
and the whirling dervish on the end of it,
the man duly managed to surface
and resolutely drag the thing inshore.

Finally man and eel lay beached
in the shallows of the bay,
each gathering strength for the final fling,
each needing to ensure the battleground
was in *his* element: the eel's the deep sea
and the man's the land.

Tide ebbing like the sea-beast's life,
the man had the simpler strategy:
to stake it flailing to the sand
and watch it gradually strand
and fail under a bloody sun.

The sun dropped west, the tide
went back, black rocks emerged
like shark fins in the bay.
Curious children waved and called,
motioned to parents and to friends
to come and see. A small crowd gathered,
a photographer captured the moment,
a small boy dropped ice cream
in the sand and began to cry.

And the fisherman? Eventually,
still in his shiny wet-suit,
with concentration and with difficulty –
for he was not young –
he tottered up the beach
dragging his still skewered catch

and dropped it, big as himself,
but dull and almost shrinking now
from life, into an old grey van
and drove away.

It had started out
as just another hot day
in a long hot summer –
a day for a steep-sloping beach
on the Cote Sauvage, for wallowing
in Atlantic waves and keeping cool.

But now, of course, it was
just another day no longer.
Now it had entered myth and was
'the day we saw the conger'.

SMITHY COTTAGE, LUGTON

In 1850 the upland hamlet of Lugton
had four houses: a hotel, a smithy,
and two toll houses for the stage

plying from Glasgow to Kilmarnock.
Pell-mell then came – and went – ironworks,
railways, brickworks, and the present day.

Today I cannot pass that old white smithy
without thinking of two spinster aunts
who lived there once.

Artists both, smart
as two pins, even their hats
were memorable.

They used to come to us
sometimes for laughter
or for supper.

I realised they were not young
that day when one of them
failed to complete

an autumn walk with us
around the reservoir.
'We're getting on,' they said.

Above all proud of their name –
my name. 'A good Scots name,
as good as anyone's,' they said.

At ten – I think – they took me
once or twice to meetings
of the Geographical Society.

We thought we were
the bees' knees, an expression
which delighted them – and me.

Another time they took me up to town,
a special treat, for tea
at the Lady Artists' Club.

They taught us limericks as kids,
of a sort which I recall my parents
may have considered unsuitable.

Their burnside garden specialised
in blue. Delphinium and pulmonaria
had them enraptured. Me too.

They traded plant cuttings
and seedlings: lavender
and tradescantia, ageratum

and salvia transylvanica,
grape hyacinth, wild violet,
and the horticultural challenge

of meconopsis – whose mere mention
had them hyperventilating
with excited, childlike adoration . . .

Easels on the seashore, their
windswept holidays at Appin were
urgently interrupted in emergency

by car trips to Glasgow
to procure that particular range
or shade of paint

without which they could not capture
a precise Argyll watercolour sunset,
an inscape over Duror . . .

That pinky-beige corduroy
tall willowy lady – hard to imagine her
driving an army lorry in the war.

Easier to visualise the shorter, elder sister
stepping it out with long smart brolly
through the Botanic Garden

whence surreptitious sideshoots were
folded away in that innocuous umbrella
and wafted past unwary park-keepers.

Their dogs – Breughel, a favourite,
then Chudleigh, and a long line of brown-eyed
retrievers often named after artists.

In due course my small son,
also of their name,
hugely entertained them.

'Oh, let him go
upstairs,' they'd cry.
'He only wants to see

if the tap in the bathroom
is dripping yet!' It was,
he would seriously announce,

to howls of indulgent laughter.
'Of course it drips.' And in the car,
later, with wide eyes he'd report,

'I think they both sleep
in one big bed – together.'
'Well, it's cold weather,'

I said. 'People of that age
are bound to feel the cold.
They keep each other warm.

'And anyway,' I added,
warming to my point, 'you
sometimes sleep with mum and me . . .'

Such zest they had and empathy;
such zany sharpness,
such delight in little things –

my filmstar dowagers,
last duchesses,
time-honoured friends.

HOW DO I WRITE A POEM?

Often like this.

Act I

I take a long evening walk.
After a time it gets dark
and my body picks up a rhythm
as words and snatches of phrases,
idioms and puns and wordgames
start shooting star-like in my head.

Sometimes I start to get lucky
and pick up coagulations –
patterns, sentences, sequences,
and I play around with these,
like any astronomer. Words
find each other, bombard
one another like atoms
in a lab experiment. Shards
and odd fragments come together
and coalesce. I'd grow crystals
if I were a chemist, or cultures
if I was discovering penicillin.

It is then that I sometimes think :
'Was that the makings
of a poem or three? Is this
to be one of those evenings?'

More often than not, it's not.
So I think no more about it.

Act II

Sometimes, later on at night,
after a bath or some other work,
I sit down with pen and paper
and revisit the mental sequences
that accompanied my walk.

Semi-legibly, often in no kind of order,
I slam them down on the page.
Then I leave them, and go to bed,
and sleep the sleep of the just.

Act III

Later, maybe next morning,
or after some weeks or months,
I may return to my scribbles,
recalling the rhythms and feelings
that accompanied my walk
of last night or of weeks ago.

If they still give a positive charge
(i.e. if I've not forgotten them),
I will then type out my scribbles,
turn the odd cliché through ninety degrees,
filleting as I go. Then begins
to emerge the skeleton of a poem.

Act IV

Act Four is to read the draft
to a group of critical listeners.
They tell me if I'm saying anything
to them. If they start to go on
about the form of the poem,
I know I'm on a hiding to nothing –
the medium has fogged the expression.

Best advice if this happens: bin it.

Act V

Last phase of all:
I sometimes try and get the poem printed
in a book or magazine. Occasionally
I am successful. Usually
I forget who I've sent the damn thing to,
but nowadays I try
to be a little more methodical
in my poetical efforts.

Coda. A Non-Government Health Warning

The time and motion folk
will be horrified to know
that for every poem of mine
to complete this curious course,
twenty fall at the first hurdle.
Two or three progress as far
as the back of a misplaced envelope,
or fall down behind a drawer,

or get shoved into some forgotten place.
One in ten makes it as far as Act Four.

A wriggling sperm has more chance
of being the lucky one
that gets to transform
the waiting ovum
than one of my poems has
to see the light of print.

So what? That
doesn't bother me too much –
nor stop me doing it.

NOTES

AYRSHIRE RECESSIONAL Sequence of poetry written after my mother's death in December 1996. In addition to feelings of bereavement, it grapples with my realisation of the loss of geographical roots. My mother was the last family link with the place where I grew up. [page 1]

HARPERCROFT A farm on Dundonald Hill. As a youngster I figured – perhaps romantically – that it took its name in the middle ages from lands feued to the harpers whose job was to entertain the nearby court at Dundonald Castle. [page 1]

THE BARNS O AYR BURN WEEL A reference to an episode recorded by Blind Harry, Sir Walter Scott and others. Tradition had it that Sir William Wallace saw the distant fire from the vantage point of Barnweil – so named, according to some, because of the Patriot's reputed comment that the Barns of Ayr (with English soldiers imprisoned inside) 'burn weel'. The nineteenth-century tower was a Victorian monument commemorating this story from the Scottish wars of independence. [page 4]

SWAN LAKE Ornamental stretch of water in the gardens of Culzean Castle, near Maybole, a haven for birdlife and a favourite place for walking. [page 5]

SKEAGH-BUSH Fairy bush (from Irish Gaelic). In Ireland, rural thorn trees, wells, and raths (mounds) often have supernatural associations with the wee folk. [page 12]

FRONT SQUARE and the READING ROOM The references are to Trinity College Dublin, where I was an undergraduate in 1963. Old Bartkus was my landlord, and he occasionally bought me a pint, especially after he'd had a successful day at the Leopardstown racecourse. [page 15]

ST LEONARDS Inner-city area of Edinburgh facing across the spectacular cliffscape of Salisbury Crags and Arthur's Seat. Completion of this recitation piece in 1992 was provoked by news that part of Edinburgh's civic millennial effort is to be the construction of a dinosaur museum at the foot of the Crags. There has also been a suggestion for carving a sort of Mount Rushmore rogues' gallery on the face of the Crags themselves, but that would call for a much sharper poetic response. [page 32]

LANGON, BESLÉ, SAINT-JUST Villages in the Pays de Redon, in the southern part of Brittany. [pages 48–53]

COTE SAUVAGE The coast between Piriac-sur-Mer and Le Croisic in Brittany, parts of which are very rocky. [page 56]

LUGTON Village in north Ayrshire. The italicised information at the beginning is from the *Third Statistical Account of Ayrshire* (1951). [page 57]

ACKNOWLEDGMENTS

Thanks are due to editors of newspapers, periodicals and anthologies in which versions of some of this poetry has already appeared : *West Coast Magazine*, *Lines Review*, *Markings*, *Northwords*, *Poetry Today*, *The Herald*, *Ulster Graduate*, *A Nest of Singing Birds*. Two poems from the 'Ayrshire recessional' sequence also appear in a School of Poets leaflet (entitled *Retrospective*, 1998). The author acknowledges encouragement and constructive criticism from fellow members of the School of Poets in Edinburgh.